HALF/MASK

AKRON SERIES IN POETRY

AKRON SERIES IN POETRY

Elton Glaser, Editor

Barry Seiler, *The Waters of Forgetting*
Raeburn Miller, *The Comma After Love: Selected Poems of Raeburn Miller*
William Greenway, *How the Dead Bury the Dead*
Jon Davis, *Scrimmage of Appetite*
Anita Feng, *Internal Strategies*
Susan Yuzna, *Her Slender Dress*
Raeburn Miller, *The Collected Poems of Raeburn Miller*
Clare Rossini, *Winter Morning with Crow*
Barry Seiler, *Black Leaf*
William Greenway, *Simmer Dim*
Jeanne E. Clark, *Ohio Blue Tips*
Beckian Fritz Goldberg, *Never Be the Horse*
Marlys West, *Notes for a Late-Blooming Martyr*
Dennis Hinrichsen, *Detail from* The Garden of Earthly Delights
Susan Yuzna, *Pale Bird, Spouting Fire*
John Minczeski, *Circle Routes*
Barry Seiler, *Frozen Falls*
Elton Glaser and William Greenway, eds., *I Have My Own Song for It: Modern Poems of Ohio*
Melody Lacina, *Private Hunger*
George Bilgere, *The Good Kiss*
William Greenway, *Ascending Order*
Roger Mitchell, *Delicate Bait*
Lynn Powell, *The Zones of Paradise*
Dennis Hinrichsen, *Cage of Water*
Sharmila Voorakkara, *Fire Wheel*
Kurt Brown, Meg Kearney, Donna Reis, Estha Weiner, *Blues for Bill: A Tribute to William Matthews*
Vern Rutsala, *How We Spent Our Time*
Clare Rossini, *Lingo*
Beckian Fritz Goldberg, *The Book of Accident*
Ashley Capps, *Mistaking the Sea for Green Fields*
Roger Mitchell, *Half/Mask*

HALF/MASK

Roger Mitchell

The University of Akron Press
Akron, Ohio

First Edition 2007
Manufactured in the United States of America.
11 10 09 08 07 5 4 3 2 1

All inquiries and permission requests should be addressed to the Publisher, The University of Akron Press, Akron, Ohio 44325-1703.

LIBRARY OF CONGRESS CATALOGING-IN-PUBLICATION DATA

Mitchell, Roger, 1935-
Half/mask / Roger Mitchell.
p. cm. — (Akron series in poetry)
Includes bibliographical references.
ISBN 978-1-931968-44-7 (pbk. : alk. paper)
I. Title.
PS3563.I82H35 2007
811'.54—dc22

2006039517

The paper used in this publication meets the minimum requirements of American National Standard for Information Sciences—Permanence of Paper for Printed Library Materials, ANSI Z39.48–1984. ∞

Cover image: Used by permission of the University of Alaska Museum of the North, catalog number UA65-007-0025, photograph by Barry J. McWayne.

The struggle for nothing, in nothing, about nothing.
—Fridtjof Nansen's description of "polar endeavour"

The scholar of one candle sees
An arctic effulgence flaring on the frame
Of everything he is.
—Wallace Stevens

For Dorian

. . . out from behind the masks has come
the part that's not quite human,
smooth stone in the river,
the part that makes
being what it is, fragile, of course,
but bearable, bearable
and unbearable,
the most beautiful part.

Contents

I

First Mask

Take that smooth rock,
the one I found out there
next to the sky,
for the middle of the forehead.
Something drifts around the mouth.
The lips go fleshy on one side
and blubber off. Thought slides through
like the tatter of a cloud.
The feather needs oiling, or replacing,
I can't tell which.
In the neighborhood of the brain,
a small smoothed fragment
of the day, rock like space.
The ear, though, should go
where the nose is, the nose
off to one side
hunting for oranges
and gossip. The smile, it
should be bigger, stupid even.
You can look like that
and still eat. You can fish
and go to the moon
on the same hook.
Part of it needs to be wood,
though bone is around.
Bits of colored glass
and an eyeball made of tar.
Tar may be hard,
so let it be chicken wire,
bluebird, a smear
of misunderstanding and dirt,
some plain scratches.
To show pleasure.
Or pain. Either one.

Sixteen Degrees

Ran yesterday at four, the sun already swallowed
        by clotted gray
overcast. Sixteen degrees, a slight film of new
        snow swirling over the road. Brisk, driven
                movements of our bodies as we try to get on
the other side
        of cold. You say nothing. I say nothing.

And the pines up Nugent Road, dark and still. No one
        around. No dog,
no truck. The crows, even the crows, their chatter mewed.
        Just the two of us, breathing the last light
                in, breathing it out, together on a dirt road
to where we are,
        brook beside us crackling under the trees.

Thule

Everything is not there, mostly. Thule itself
disputed by those who never left their desks.

The word is of no known origin, a term
for the extreme northern limit of travel

long before Pytheas of Massilius went there,
a place no comfortable Mediterranean rationalist

could afford to let in to his orderly arrangements.
"We cannot believe," goes the text,

"that a private person, who was also a poor man,
should have made such immense journeys."

Strabo would repeat Polybius, Strabo
whose forty-three volumes of *Historical Commentaries*

live on only in fragments quoted by later
and less consequential commentators, passers-on

of opinion, proven and repeated, proven
by being repeated, come to canonical sclerosis

by being around, always and quoted, a thing
made of saying, made of wanting to sound plausible.

Anyway, who could have countenanced a place
that is "neither unmixed land or sea or air,

nothing but a compound of all three?" Pytheas
straining his quill to pull it out of his memory.

Think of jellyfish, he said. *Pulmo marinus.*
"An acaleph of the etenophera," said one

unhelpful footnoter who would not allow himself
"earth and sea and everything else held

in suspense, through which one can neither
walk nor sail." Someone has checked *The History*

of Greek Literature out of the library forever.
When I point that out at the front desk,

I get that Alexandrine sag in the flesh
you see on those who have lived too long

at the edge of disorder. You can have a world,
it says, but only if the world wants it.

We have not yet burned the place to the ground,
though if we did, we would still want there to be

a word, and, therefore, a place
where "the extreme limit of travel

and discovery" lives, the "highest and uttermost
point or degree attained or attainable,

the acme, the limit," earth and sea and everything
so thick you could not walk or drive your car

or anymore be comfortable in your being
or be anything but rolling, blubbered, and amazed.

Above Bow Lake

Tatters of the melting glacier
fling themselves over the edge.
Water thrashes in the brook below,
a live snake on a skillet. Beside us,
working upstream against the current,
a dipper, no bigger than a robin,
the color of darkness in daytime,
of sky about to storm. We stand,
our faces turned up, spray
that may have fallen as snow
ten thousand years ago on our tongues.

Dream Seed

On a stretch of landscape on the north end of Harris, a cluster of hills and rock, cast in one of the grays the sea makes on a cloudy day. It has not seen the sea since that day millions of years ago, which was millions of years before anything remotely human could be, when the island came up out of the water. Even today only a few stunted bushes and pinched clusters of moss and grass cram into the creases of the rock where a few grains of dirt managed somehow not to be blown or washed away. Somewhere near the beginning of time, thrown back onto a planet as yet incapable of us, here is life that was possible before our own. Sunlight and rain. Rock packed in grasses. Wind shaking the seeds out of clusters of tiny flowers. Seeds suddenly in flight, ignorant and delirious, grabbing at the air.

The Stones at Callinish, Isle of Lewis

A boarded-up hotel beside
a fishing pier, a pub. Above them both,
a church crouched on a hill. Whoever brought
Christ to this desolate coast did it
with sword and fire, and it's not clear today
whether it took, or whether the slow seep
of centuries, the long winter nights,
would ever let anything be that wasn't
as sullen as the hill. The village
is that way, too. When you step outside,
there it is, the universe, all of it,
the glare of it pure, God's unshaven face
so close your skin rasps. Whoever raised
these stones did a good job of vanishing, too,
though the longer I stand here, the more
it seems it was deeper into the genes
they went, not just into the air.

Museum

On Duckworth Street, stuffed,
the last Newfoundland wolf
in a glass case, its fur a mottled gray
like much of the rock here, nudging
the lush, stunted spruce and fir,
grasses thickened with moss.
Long rangy legs for traveling,
eyes that, if they had little warmth
and no sentimentality,
had neither complaint nor venom.

A few miles to the east, Cape Spear,
the tip, the actual point itself,
thrust out like a tongue
at the raw Atlantic.

A blowup of an old photograph
of St. John's harbor, backdrop
to a small arrangement of things
I now can't recall. Utterly other,
the three-masted whaler leans
at the slip in centuries of grime,
the dock hidden under stacks of lumber,
barrels of fish and whale oil,
men with thick hands, leathery,
and no sense at all that anyone watches,
that a century later someone
would see them and, knowing
nothing about them, think
this was the world he came from.
Not a world made for the viewer
or one to be strolled through,

nothing was done to it
to show what the past was like.
There was no past, nothing
but the need to outwit
the moment, to bring down again
the prey of another night in bed.

Doing Ninety

We are driving across southern Alberta on our way to Saskatchewan. It is the end of July in a year of rainy excess, though today the sky has nothing in it but sunlight. The wheat is tall, thick, and dark green. Both the rapeseed and the flax are in bloom, a sharp taxi yellow and a blue you could anchor all the blues to, the blue to which all other blues belong. All we have to do is keep the pedal down and the car aimed. The road does the rest. The land barely moves. It takes a whole horizon's worth of it to rise and fall, and that only a few feet at a time. The last town we passed was twenty miles back, a cluster of fifteen houses set back from the highway, a gas station, a motel, and a coffee shop. The next town is another twenty miles away. Another cluster of houses parked next to the highway. Otherwise, all we see are fields, a farm every four or five miles, an occasional car, and here and there a tree. The fields grow right down to the road. Every inch in grass. Views that go as far as sight can on the surface of the earth. And the land undulating vaguely like sea in a beginning wind. I look down at the dashboard, and I'm doing ninety. I've never done ninety in my life, and now that I'm doing it, it feels like nothing. Floating, maybe. I'm moving, but were I to move like this all day, I'd still be here, drifting on a sea of grass.

Crocus, Beginning

Something like rain moving across space, drift of matter,
  tiny flurry,
as they say of snow. Falling. Though, as there is no
  down as yet, or up, falling is only
    a sliding from here to there of a thing that changed
mass or its thrust
  and could not stay what it was, where it was.

Where things are seems to be what they are, as in shadow
  or light. But then
nothing can stay where (be what) it is for long.
  A thing has to come in, and, for an in,
    there must be an out. Maybe things are nothing
but wake: long, thin
  contrails dissolving sky into heaven.

Though why the substance I'm calling rain, thing named for what
  it does (not is),
decided to move out of the silence, into
  the accidental, maybe the crocus
    can tell us, shivering there in its second spring,
November's pale
  reminder of the first tethering to.

Lichen

In the long history of uses, known and suspected,
experts speak of the "folklore," Egyptians who,
for "medicinal purposes" in the eighteenth century
before Christ, put against the skin *evernia furfuracea,*

or into the exposed orifices of their kings
and the queens and cats chosen to accompany them
on the slow journey to the world beneath this one,
dried extract of another of the twenty thousand species.

Hippocrates thought *usnea barbarata* good
for "uterine trouble," and the Chinese the usnea
longissima as expectorant. The Mayans
still battle the common cold with an usnea tea.

For the more intransigent ailments, *mucus cranii*
humanii, lichen grown on the human skull.
Though it "cost its weight in gold," a pinch of it
relieved the racking of catarrhal hemoptysis.

"Cough-tea" or "lichen-chocolate" eased
the wrenchings of the bronchial root tree
brought on by the tubercle bacillus. Keats
may have sipped *Cladonia* above the Spanish Steps.

Fever, jaundice, epilepsy, gout, edema,
convulsions of every sort thrown at this dense, low-lying plant,
which, since it knew how to grow on rock
and in climates hostile to human life, must,

they thought, have powers beyond hallucinogens,
beyond emetics and poisonous mushrooms,
blood-rallyers and sight-stabilizing molds.
Place a compress, they said, of fresh lichen on a new

or infected wound. If starving in the Arctic,
make a tea of it, boiling it in snow if you can't
find water. The lichen, though, or maybe the starving,
brings on violent convulsions, cramps, and nausea.

If starving in the Arctic, they said,
lie with your back to the wind, your knees drawn up.
Wait. And when you can wait no longer, stop waiting.
See, it says it right here. Stop. Be deliberate and slow.

After that it says nothing.

Mask on Mask

Today I put on the mask of looking
out the window and seeing the one crow
drink out of a puddle in the driveway.
It walks into the shadow of the stripped
black locust sprawled across the bright green grass,
which is a mask itself called pretending
it is spring and the leaves are only sleeping.

Everything waits for whatever winter
wants. A few more days, apparently,
out there in the air somewhere tossing thought
into the sky and letting it drift off
quietly in its own goony mask, the sun.

The Deaths of William Braine

Look at the face. His, one of three corpses
they went all that way to dig up, one for whom
a descendant somewhere in the west of England
flew to the disinterment on his own.
His last gasp preserved, as if he had died
yesterday. Just the shirt gives him away.
His coffin might, as well, joined by a craft
so exact one would have to go to school
to learn the terms. And who still binds big toes
together with torn bedsheet or shirttail?
No one is sure why they abandoned ship,
shuffled along the coast, dying piecemeal,
driven to hacking their dead into chunks
of meat, which they carried, boiled, in the boots
of the same. Bones have begun to show up,
screened, measured, in the scientific journals,
photos of fibulas along which the tiny
knife nicks still stand out after a hundred
and fifty winters in the open. Yes,
they were still able, at his death, to bury
their dead, still sure they had come to this place
for a reason. Though some were starting to drop
their reflexes, others dragged down into fogs
of fatigue so deep they could not sleep free of it.
And so could neither hunt nor cart, could not
stand for long, leaned against the ship's gunwhales
or one another till they leaned so far out
they fell. Where we find them among the fears
of surviving relatives, all dead, of course,
in stories told by Inuit hunters
for generations, hunters who stood by
when they passed, listless, could not help without

dying themselves. The distant descendant looks
down at the face in the box, the teeth bared
in a greeting, a smile like a blow to the head.
He says something we can't quite hear, steps back.
The lid is hammered into place again.

White Winged Swarming

1

Sunday.
Only a few crows this morning.
A treeful of starlings
down by the road.
I walk up past
a hill of old tires
and out onto
the rolling plateaus
of sandy waste,
thinking of those
who left their ships
locked in ice
and set out across
continents of snow
with a single thought,
who ate their dogs,
one by one, who pulled
the sled themselves.
And of the ones
who found them, the tiny
separated teeth,
tins of perfectly
preserved pears.
Across a small ravine,
a scree of stoves,
torn bags, things
I can't make out,
the usual stuff.
At home, for hours,
I look for the hint
of dead animal,

rotted fruit.
I lift my sleeve
to my face
several times,
hugging it to me.

2

I'm up on the dump again,
looking at things.
This isn't a Romantic dump
or a Classical one.
It's the dump at the edge
of town, the one where the road
flashes on the other side
of a few spindly trees
and the cars go by
and don't stop.
It's the one where they took
the old rug from the basement
and the box full of jars
saved for a life
you were sure
you were going to live.
Your radio with the bent
aerial and the dust
is up there, too,
and the stuff
you couldn't do without
all those years.
It's up there,
buried in a shallow grave.
Two gulls tear
at a chicken wing.
A third one screams.
I pull at a piece
of old plastic bag.

I pull and pull,
but I don't come
to the end of it.
It rips open the wound
in the ground
and shows me . . . well,
you know what it shows me.
We were both there
when it happened,
when the earth started
spitting us back.

3

It's a good place to study
the behavior of certain birds.
And if you look hard,
you can see the world up there,
the heap we make
with our caring and not caring.
It's all there,
crows thrown over it
like crumbs of a burnt cake.
The gulls scream something
I can't make out.
When I move closer,
when I try to get
right up into their feather
and flap, when I try to keep
this blackened bit
of banana to myself,
tossing it back
to the back of my throat,
gnashing it down
at a gulp, they hop away.
Not far,
just to the next

scratched-over place in the sand,
where, sleepy but alert,
they wait for the next
spasm of need,
truckload of plastic,
crushed grease.

4

And I go into the store
and I think, here
is where it starts.
I handle the little item
in its smooth plastic bubble.
I rub the bubble,
soft as a newborn skull.
I know a crow
who wants to pick through
these glazed arrangements
of salt. I know a gull
who sits on a lamp post
waiting. And here I am
scavenging the aisles,
looking for something prenatal,
wrapped in my own bubble.

5

I knew it would happen.
Not where or how or when,
but I knew it would.
I didn't know it,
but I knew it.
It's hard to explain.

Something would break.
You know,
some little thing.

And there it would be,
broken forever.

And I would give my life to it.
I would not understand it,
and I would have
no name for it.
But I would give
everything to it.
Not knowing it
at first, but doing it.

There was no other way.
There was to have been
no other way.

Everything
and the giving
of everything
to it.

6

How I love these gulls,
even the stealing
from one another.
They have left
their old home, the sea,
to follow the veins
of garbage, inland.
Up there on the hill,
the bulldozer
backs and fills
under a cloud of them.
I call it a cloud.
It's more like a
scrambling flutter.

Above that,
up where the true clouds are,
a strange wheeling, slow.
A gathering, perhaps,
before a departure.
A whispering, out of range,
about the old ways,
about the new.
I stand and watch it,
longing to go,
longing to be gone.

7

Which gull is it
that never sees
the land? Have I
imagined it,
out there riding
the swells or hung
on a long hook
of wind? The world
of the gull is nearly
the world itself,
but this gull sits
on a solitary hump
of sea, a rolling
shrug of the universe,
and waits. This gull
mates forever.
To wind, water,
sun, and rain.
To the one gull
that finds her.
They make a nest
of themselves
in the curve

between two waves.
And their mating,
no one has seen.
It is done aloft,
at night, and may take
years. Years
circling in the dark,
wingtip
brushing wingtip.
The young ride
on their mother's back
until they can fly,
and then leave.
The father
has left already.
And the mother.
She is the last,
but she leaves, too.
It is not known
if the young survive,
or whether perhaps
these are the kind
who leave their species,
who live where nothing
is fixed, where stillness
glides over great deeps.
We have to rely
on the odd sighting,
people, boatbound
and lonely, who,
in a world shrunk
to the world itself,
need to believe
they have been there,
that being there
is being itself.

8

The highway holds the curve
of the river close.
A land form rises to the right,
skims along a flank
of glacial frieze, and there,
halfway up, a white,
winged swarming. By now,
I know the signs, raw scrape
in the ground, relentless gulls.
Too far into this scheme
of feeding, of having to be
someone, of having to think
my way toward morning,
of reaching the day's end
somewhere I wasn't at dawn,
dragged by a harsh, migratory
urge across a rake of clean,
hard, unforgiving ideas,
I give it my birdy,
sideways eye, and drive on.

The Other Side of the Air

They say that the animals hunted in the Arctic want to be caught and killed. But only by the best hunters, the most skillful and patient. I only repeat what I've been told, but they apparently lie around in the slack times and compare reputations, as we would makes and models of cars. This is to say that the caribou and the seals and the musk ox think exactly like the hunters. In fact, they speak the same language. It is difficult sometimes to tell them apart, one so carefully imitates the other, right down to the verb tenses. When it comes time to go up into the other world, which is what the bears and the ptarmigans and the others call the place the hunters live in, they say it is only on the other side of the air. You cannot imagine the uses to which we are put, they say to one another. Every part of me will be devoured, some by the mouth, some by the eye. I plan to give myself to———(and here the great seal mentions a famous name in the village). The other seals are impressed. They snort and bark and roll from side to side on their huge fatty torsos. He's a good one, they say. Yes, the great seal says, he took my mother two years ago and now wears her to hunt in. It was a great fight. I will make him work just as hard. I will make him think he will not get me. I will make him think he will die, that his children will starve. But then I will come back to him a little ways, but very carefully so he will not be able to tell it, and turn so he can do it swiftly. Oh, he will be proud of himself. What lucky ones we are, to make such happiness merely by dying.

You Look Out

across cornstubble near the White River.
Except for the trees along the banks,
you'd think you were somewhere above Peel Strait
where permafrost cups summer snowmelt.

Awake again in the middle of the night,
I'm reading Nansen. He's reached the Sea
of Amur, locked himself, his ship, and crew
in the ice. Come summer,
he will dash out with the dogs
and be the first to reach the pole.

Alone and far away, remote, a step
or two beyond human, real being.

For a year you sit in a small boat
wondering why you agreed
to do exactly that. The only sound
is the dogs barking on deck, whirr
of the windmill driving the electric
generator, groan of the hull
twisting to free itself from the icegrip.

Yesterday, a long, rainy drive
into the city. I kept passing
the same car, an Acura, red. It kept
passing me. In all those hundreds, one car.
A formation of some kind, we swooped low
over the ground, up the hill on 38th,
it on past the graveyard and art museum,
me down onto the floodplain of the White River,
spillway of the interstate,

and back to the life I was barely
paying attention to, crows over bare
branches, spatter of rain turning to snow
on the windshield, and the small gathering
we were about to make for Jim, whose life
he now wanted back from all
that twenty years of work had taken from him.

I look out over the crisscross of paths
between this building and the next,
the brick walkways, leafless branches
like a net above them, and between them,
the half-hurried urgency of people on their way.
This morning a walk up through a small patch
of brick-laned wilderness, the woods kept here
in town to remind us of the first life
of this place. Sun glistened on the bricks.
Nansen, of course, would not make it.

I know now that I don't want another life,
other than the one I have.
It has an easy isolation to it,
enough of a boreal lassitude
to keep us looking beyond the trees.
In the evening, we listen to the hiss
of the steamer on the wood stove.
Nothing happens for hours.
We could be locked in ice ourselves,
drifting toward the pole.
We might make a run for it.
Tomorrow. Or next year.
Deep in the hold, the pages turn.

In the Art Museum Coffee Shop

the spindly metal furniture of a Parisian park.
Of the sort I saw once in a photo,
Gertrude and Alice sitting
under the shade of some trees
with Bravig Imbs, Aix-les-Bains, 1927.

At the top of the stairs,
above the arboretum,
voices flutter out
into the latticed space,
come back a little rubbed,
a little enlarged.

I remember the purity and force
of the song of the white-throated sparrow
trapped in the Biodome in Montreal.
We had come up for the day,
walked along the docks in the cold sunshine
and watched the jugglers for a while
and the unicyclists.
Then went into one of those shops
along the rue or the allée,
shops made up entirely for us,
people who mark the stages of their life,
when they find them, with tokens.
Or if they haven't found them, or aren't sure,
mark them anyway, pauses
like ledges along a mountain path.

Mine, a small gray soapstone loon
with its head thrown back like a coyote,
which you did not want me to know

you had bought when you bought it
and then gave me months later.

The sun struggles this morning.
From the sound of the banging behind me,
so does the maker of cappuccinos.
I think of him as a graduate student in fine arts
whose work will one day fill a barn in a meadow,
but today he does the work
for which he does not sense he will be grateful
toward the end of his life.

The first thing I see
in the room at the top of the stairs
stares back at me.
"Mask for a Mummy Bundle," the tag says,
and where there would be eyes,
two luminous white shells,
two moons of the sea.

I went back for another look,
as I was trying to write about it,
and though the facts often don't matter,
I want to say I had forgotten
the narrow aquiline nose, eyebrows
in bas-relief, and the small mouth,
just as I had forgotten when
exactly it was you gave me the loon.
It may be what we recall that counts,
that survives, as Pound said,
but I think it must be what we forget
that we are.

Last Three Minutes

One day the galaxies will go
back into their own shadow,

disappear into space and time,
taking both with them,

the stars and all return to be
the "singularity"

they once were.

Who knows what it was, or will be?
A wide and shoreless sea,

sound that nothing makes,
dream-driven mathematics,

winds that blow against themselves,
black light, mouthless vessels?

Whatever's other.

II

Grise

(pronounced "grease")

It was almost summer, late July, when bay ice
cracks like gunshot with the tide's rising and falling,
sea breaking its mold. This was Ellesmere, northernmost
island in the Arctic archipelago, twin
almost to Greenland, place where the sun vanishes
in winter, merely spins overhead in summer.
Fog over Grise, thick layers of it, made the pilot
swing out over the fiord to the west, then bank
eastward between two cliffs it seemed both wings might brush
as we passed between them. A tight corkscrew descent
through the fog brought the airstrip up, a slab
no more than the given gravel of a glacial floodplain,
rearranged slightly, tilted, upslope for landing,
downslope for takeoff. The new terminal building,
small, yellow with blue trim, a stretch of chain link fence:
gestures toward the world we'd come from. A few people
had come up from the hamlet to see what cargo,
human and otherwise, the week's one flight had brought
to their isolated world. Though that term is mine,
not theirs. Whatever isolation is, it has
an airstrip just outside of town, cable
in every house, candy bars, tee shirts, ATVs,
all the paraphernalia of what's called there,
The South. In this place, where the bones of the world
still showed, it was strange to be checked out by a knot
of young boys, leaning on a railing, smoking,
in baseball caps. It could have been Bloomington.
One of the older men walked toward, then past me, eyes
averted, as though the measure of a person
could be taken by smell or a pass at close range.
I stood in a blaze of hydrochloric light,

waiting to see what they would do with my pack frame
and whether I should walk down into the hamlet,
or climb aboard the truck for a ride to the lodge
and a dinner already prepared for us.

I had come alone. The years reading about it
had finally landed me on a kind of ground—
tundra, polar desert—where the machinery
of creation—volcano, glacier, water, wind—
almost erased the dreams people made of these things.
Three of the passengers, I learned, formed an "eye team,"
ophthalmologists from Ottawa, here to check
the sight of the children and try to persuade them
to wear their glasses. One of the doctors, Marc,
said you had to convince them, the boys anyway,
that glasses would make them better hunters.
Only then would they wear them and only for that
reason. Two days later, I would be asked to praise
the fresh kill, a ring seal, of a ten-year-old boy,
he and his friend eager to show me, a stranger,
what they had done, what they could do. He pulled the limp
form from a garbage bag, its head a bloody pulp.
It was a baby, he said, only four feet long.
I took one of its flippers in my hand, felt
a familiar, complicated bone structure
under the wet fur. Congratulations, I said.
What will you do with it? Eat it, was his answer.
That same evening, out for a stroll along the shore,
a stony beach where the tide had stranded chunks
of the ice breaking up in the bay, I saw a man
carve the carcass of a seal, laid out on a block
of ice, into long, thick steaks of the rose-gray flesh.
His wife, two children, me, an audience of four,
marveling at the perfect flesh, perfectly cut,
dropping in an orderly heap, slap on wet slap.

A reservation at the lodge gave me no clue
what to expect: meals, a bed, perhaps a shower.
I had to be able to carry everything,
long distances perhaps. I had a fear, I think,
of being alien. And why not; I was.
That was the whole idea, in a way. To go
where human life, my kind at least, had a loose fit.
The north is tricky, though, the draw of it largely
its stories and legends, many easily
reinforced by an image—iceberg, bear, white wind.
Images of overmastering fact, where fact
would seem to strip life of desire, willfulness, dream,
all the baggage humans heap on astonished earth.
But then, the Rome we know, the Rome we want to know,
is a Rome the Italians must grow weary of,
and the Inuit long ago said to the world
they were through playing noble or happy savage
in the West's tales of necessary innocence.
When I stepped out of the plane onto the ground,
I could barely see, the sun and the wound-up light
of my preconceptions brighter than mirrored fire.

It could have been Bloomington if it had had
thirty-one pizza parlors and fourteen quarries.
If a gilt fish flew at the top of the restored
courthouse. Or if anyone there recalled Rapp's. Rapp's
Pizza Train, the Nutcracker Suite, nude swimming
in Griffy reservoir. We would know we were near home
if May's Greenhouse were just south of town and just south
of it the Blue Light Lounge had gone back to being
a used car lot. It could have been Bloomington if
a student swam through the sewers under the whole

of Bloomington. It might have been Faris Market,
Krogers. Or what about Hays, the Runcible Spoon.
Not to mention American Futon, the Old
Library, the even older library, where
the Farmers' Market crammed into the parking lot
each Saturday and that mild bearded man, wearing
a pork pie hat, peddled stuff we'd never seen at
prices we couldn't believe. A fiddler bucked tunes
in the sun while his wife kept time slapping a stick
against a board. Where did they go when the day died?
They and the others, where did they hang the hours up?
Out at the Porthole? Out at the lake where the cook
on a slow night came out from her greasy precinct
and, to the mellifluous local rhythms of
The Nightriders skipping about on "Rockytop,
Tennessee," played the spoons against her thigh. Now that,
not only could have been Bloomington, but was. This
was an altogether other, and similar, thing.

To have no way out of this geological
cul-de-sac, wash of treeless stone crowded against
the coast by steep talus fallen off the cliff face,
nothing but a costly flight, one you might take once
in a lifetime, at the end of it, say, perhaps
never, perhaps content always in all weathers
to look at the bay, land sloped evenly down
to a beach of small stones, shingle, rocks offshore,
high mountain to the right, guarding the westerly
approaches of the wind, another to the north,
Devon in the distance, across Jones Sound, giver
and taker, you and your family forever,
here on this island which you sometimes walk up
into to look back at the sea, at the glaciers
pouring into it off Devon, but mostly so

you can look out over the icefield at the top
of the world, sheet of perpetual white, sister
to the sea, mother, though no one crosses it, and
of a stranger silence than any rock, any air.

Except, of course, winter when the islands are locked
together as a single continent of ice,
across which you might ride forever or as long
as you can carry the means to keep on moving.
Or until you reach the floe edge where whales beckon
in the spring and the currents mark the edge
of the universe which you long across for the
islands where moss thickens rock, rock accompanies
stars in their falling, and caribou at last rest.
And all this in the dark or with the moon spooling
out of the sky, and but for an occasional
stillness, wind slicing air into thin strands of glass.

From there not only might you have forty or more
words for snow, but as many also for darkness,
time, the varieties of wind, windlessness, woe,
movement of cloud, kinds of cloudlessness, vagaries
of shadow and thought: looming, ecstatic, shapely.
You might call water by hundreds of its moods. As,
water into which a stone has been thrown, water
the color of water surrounding a rock, rock
near the sea's edge, azure or blue, water that lies
flat in the distance, pale water, water hidden
under ice, water cloudy from the sky, water
cloudy from carrying dust down from beneath
the grinding of glaciers, sweet water, strong water,
water that holds ten-foot-thicknesses of ice up
off the sea's floor, water that drowns ice, wrinkled water,
water sliding sideways, water lapping shyly

at small stones, teasing water, mists and mirages,
water over land, standing, water we came from,
water we can't go back to, water we will, wild
white froth, trickles, spills, muddy water, mud itself,
meltwater, spring water, no water, boat dragged up
on the shore, flood, boat at the bottom of the sea.

Up at six that morning, silence abounding,
my bed no more than fifty feet from shore, the ground
held up in front by a row of rusted oil drums
filled with gravel, the tide crowding the wreckage
of the winter's ice against the bay, light still light,
but creamy, as though mixed with night and memory,
still, if light can be still, casting the broad shadow
of the mountain behind the hamlet over it,
I skipped breakfast (I could eat later) to go find
the ancient Thule Culture site I was told
lay to the west, past the airstrip and the dump, beyond
the new sewage lagoon, hacked through the permafrost.
As I passed the airstrip, I saw something I'd missed
when we landed, my mind full of the moment,
a small graveyard, outlined in white stones, twenty-five
crosses in all, a small number for the nearly
fifty years, since the old times, people had lived here.
But there, at six in the morning, two little girls
draped over a cross, whispering, did not see me
passing, deep as they seemed to be in coaxing back
into the world some trace of the person buried there.
I thought I heard an answer, but to what question,
the silence could not say. And then, they spotted me,
came running, shouting, "What's your name?" and "Do you have
any candy?" No, I said, I'm sorry. "Have you any
chips?" No, no food, I said. "Orange, apple?"

I asked them who was buried there. Come see, they said.
Tookillkeek Iguktak was one, and on her grave,
as on the others, small coins, necklaces, a stone
or two. Josephie Kiguktak had collected
cigarette lighter, twist of blue wire, fishing bobs,
two erasers. Ooleesee Akeogak, "Mom"
spelled out in plastic roses, a faded quilt spread
at her feet, had three earrings, five pacifiers,
more blue wire, a gold ring. When you visit the dead,
they said, you must leave something behind, anything,
and no one must disturb these gifts, even the stones,
the twists of wire, the bit of string, perhaps these thoughts.
Who were these people? The girls seemed not to hear
my question or were struck by a sudden shyness
or hunger, and ran off downhill to the hamlet,
leaving me with other voices, similar ghosts,
the foundational story, Grise's shadowed past.

The testimony presented to the Royal
Commission on Aboriginal Peoples,
those involved in the High Arctic Relocation,
from the hamlets of Pond Inlet (North Baffin Island)
and Inukjuak (formerly Port Harrison)
in Arctic Quebec to (or near) Resolute Bay,
where a fully equipped air base flourished, and to
Grise Fiord where there was in the words of those "dumped"
there ("dumped" being their word) "absolutely," this
being their term as well, "nothing," came first from them,
"relocatees," as they were called, remembering
in 1993 that first winter when no
sun shone, 1953, bonds of family
and place broken, for no reason made clear to them,
they now called upon to tell their story out

in hopes that never again would such winds batter
and never, given the reach of the great oral
memory of the Inuit, would they be forgot.
They testified in Inuktitut, a language
so spread out and localized across the Arctic
one group has trouble understanding another's
version of it. The translators had to move fast
to get it down as they spoke. Forty years, but still,
the images vivid, the memories intact.

Minnie Allakariallak said, "They were told,
'you have to leave to another community.
The government wants you to move.'
When Qallunat spoke, we were afraid of them."
She said, "They were separated
from those whom they loved so much
and would never see again."
She said, "They had absolutely no idea
where they were going."

Markoosie Patsuak said, "The land
they were living in before had been their land
for many hundreds of years.
No one thought about leaving."

Rynie Flaherty said, "There was no vegetation,
just bare rock and large boulders." She said,
"They were merely dumped on the shore."

Samwillie Elijasialak said, "It is not the habit
of the Inuit to write about unpleasant things."
Besides, "they could only send letters once a year,"
when the supply ship came.

Mary Attagutaluk said, "The white man
treats Inuit like they treat their dogs.
The Inuit are told to sit, so they sit, and become silent."

Anna Nungak said, "They were taken to a place
where there was absolutely nothing.
They saw the ship sailing away.
They stayed in tents all year."

Rynie Flaherty again: "In the spring,
there was no flour, no milk, no sugar.
She could only feed her little son small pieces of seal meat."

Larry Audlaluk said, "His mother, in despair,
used to ask questions to no one.
'Where are the animals? Where the fish?'"

Sarah Amagoalik said, "They used to go to the dump
because the aircraft used to dump a lot of good food.
The police was the doctor. There were doctors
at the base, but the police told them
not to come around, not to treat the Inuit.
The only medicine the police gave was juice."

Elizabeth Allakariallak said, "She remembers oranges,
the excitement of finding oranges in the dump."

John Amagoalik said, "He remembers scrounging, too.
Whenever an airplane arrived, they would all go to the dump.
They knew that leftover sandwiches would be thrown away
in the dump, some half eaten."

Martha Flaherty said, "She still remembers the trip,
when the children all had their hair cut off,
without permission, without consultation with the parents.

She fought against this," though she was only three,
"and the doctor ran after her with scissors in his hand."

Maina Arragutainaq said, "That year, her sister
lost her mind. They took her out by plane,
never heard of her again."

Lizzie Amagoalik said, "After they returned
to Inukjuak, twenty-six years later, no one recognized them.
The people they had known were all dead.
They were strangers now in their old country."

Susan Salluviniq said, looking around the room,
"The children now are the caretakers of the pain
of their parents, in the move to Resolute Bay
and Grise Fiord."
                                   The voices slid to a low rumble,

a guttural motion in the bay below, sea
clearing its throat of the ice, as if it would speak,
as if what it had to say might echo the cries
of the six ravens arranged on its broken back.

Six ravens arranged on the broken back of the sea.
Six reasons to think the ravens good company.
Six querulous gargles, as many hacked squawks.
In this, a dry cold haven where even rock talks.

Let us praise dumps. Human slash, breeding ground of rats,
middens to an age of industrial excess,
cancer of affluence, all these, yet also sites
of second and third chances, forms of forgiveness

available to things, useless things, broken, things
that never worked in the first place, this the second
and better place, scrap heap, where scrappiness itself
thrives, where you can climb aboard a wrecked snowmobile
and come away with knob, fender, piston rod, wire,
or go instead to the stacks of used lumber, crates,
to pry them apart so they might serve again, some
doghouse, shelf, child's dogsled, some happiness forming
slowly in a father's mind. I can't imagine
what they'll do with the oil tank, big as a boxcar,
but already graffiti have appeared there, crude,
to be sure, but there the junk of language might sing
songs we thought were noises, sculptures appear where rust
only, unnatural lichen, grows. May no dump
be what it was to the ancestors of this place,
a thing they needed to survive, but may they piece
new things out of its infinite variety,
use, as all our ancestors did, everything up.

It's 10 P.M. and just offshore two men in a boat
pull up a net. Something sullen pulls against them.
First one seal, then another, both badly tangled
in the net, both drowned, tumble into the boat, one
with a wide bite taken out of its neck, raw rose.
The men wrestle the heavy, bulbous, dark green forms
into the boat, and once freed of the net, drape them,
heads facing outward, over the gunwhales. The work
is long, but the men do it with no thought but that
of doing it. And the season cooperates,
giving them light, all night if they need it, fatigue
when the work is done. It's ten, and the light, dulled
only a little by its gesture toward the west,
pours back over the thick rafts of ice in the bay.

Johnny is rotting walrus in a shallow ditch
across the road. That's what Hene thinks, anyway.
Johnny is his English name. It's been there nearly
a year, which means it's almost ready. A small swarm
of flies (standard issue diptera) hovers
at the edges of the square of orange plastic
held to the ground by a few boards weighed down with stones.
I won't be here when they lift it out of the hole,
wipe the reeking green mold away and eat it straight,
as is, no ketchup, salt, or fork. Rot, after all,
is just a different way to break the fibers down,
cooking where there's no wood, at thirty-nine below.

I went to see the dogs today. Chained to the ground
well away from the hamlet, and chained so they can't
reach each other, they stirred at my approach, wary,
curious rather than friendly. Bones litter
the beach in front of them, ribs and femurs, walrus,
musk-ox, bear, the oddly human hand of a seal,
all of it stripped clean. I'm not their boss or a meal,
but not knowing what else to make of me, they broke
into yowls, pleading, but it seemed, too, promising
to tear me apart should I make the wrong move.
I'd love to let one of them go, see where it went,
follow it out to the end of its feral rope.
But I have my own rope to contend with, a walk
to take into the next valley, and beyond that,
the map promises a deep fiord, more stony
coastline, the broad tongue of Jackman Glacier, silence,
and, if I make it, the silence about silence.

Everywhere I went, a company of ravens.
Calling down from the cliffs, swooping ahead of me

along the coastal rocks, looping back to catch me
from behind. No migration for these birds. Winter
is as good as summer. Not quite so hot. Inclined,
says my bird book, to be solitary. Except
when inclined to pester their neighbor, or jabber,
interrogate the weather, infiltrate whatever
looks promising, unwatched or edible. Which is,
given their inclination, almost anything.
True, they stick to the boreal, the mountainous.
Forest and tundra are the same to them, both far
from man. Who needs watching, frankly, needs to be made
a little uneasy, given his less than kind
habits, his somewhat ravenous history.
A history, it seems, he would blame on the raven.
I've misplaced my dictionary of ravenspeak,
but the book of my own multifoliate tongue
(from the Anglo-Saxon *hraefn,* Danish *ravn*)
says that to seize by violence is to raven,
that a ravener is one who plunders, if not
ravishes, that from there the distance to ravage
is short, that ravening is to rave, unravel,
go mad, be rabid, finally illogical,
since to ravel is the same as to unravel.
Rave, too, being praise; a rave, controlled delirium.
Their voice a croaking CR-RUCK or PRRUK, metallic TOK.
Intelligent and mischievous, to some a god.

It's a rare mountain I don't want to walk up.
There's something about being over there, up there,
where you aren't, about getting there, being able to.
I think, too, of being at the other end of sight
and looking back. The tiny crease in the landscape
from which we've come. I don't live in a valley,
though I have. I live on a plain, glacial moraine,

a kind of gradual, mixed slanting, up and down,
along some sharp ridges, slung through a few bottoms,
in amongst sycamores, beeches, some high wide oaks.
And creeks. Bryant's Creek, Brummet's, the forks of the Salt,
plus a few hundred nameless rills, slips, dirt roads, bends
in the road, around which anything can, and does,
raise up its virtual tunnel of fine white dust.

There's no path up Greenlander. You find your own way
by scrambling up rocks that can't look much different
from the day they fell there thousands of years ago.
"Undifferentiated gneiss and granite," says
the geological map on the dining room wall,
"Precambrian," the oldest earthly stuff known.
It's at the top you find the *inuksuit,* tall cairns
in a roughly human shape, staring down at Grise,
visible once you know they're there. If we're to be
alone in the world, put on some remote strip
of bony gravel, and left there to figure things out,
a rough, artful stack of some bountiful local
material, made to tear concern for our lives
right out of the rocks, sand, trees, whatever the world
is where we are, might be good company to keep.
Once you know they're there, you see them gazing down
from several ridges, mountains, clifftops. They see you,
you say. You see them, too. Leaning—why not?—toward you.

I have two images of the place. Late July,
spring in the High Arctic, when ice starts to break up
in the bay and across Jones Sound. Summer will last
barely a month, but now, down at ground level,
and you must get down to ground level to see it,
as thick an expression of blooming, as varied,

as any wildness anywhere on earth can cram
into its square inch of geological debris.
Long blanketing mosses sprouting needled seed pods
in shades of molten ember, clusters of cream white
cloches, bladders of some veined purple campion,
the ubiquitous rag-happy arctic poppy,
tight grasses, spatters of psychedelic lichens.
The living fire burns quick and hot and everywhere.

The other is the stone, stone begun somewhere up
where the cliffs are now, that broke and fell and, falling,
kept on breaking down and now makes the dirt and grass
of the place, the ground, the small pressed pebbles, gravel
I've been calling it, though this is the stuff put down
by the earth and its rumblings over the past
fifteen thousand years, palmprint of the last glaciers.
Except at its edges here and there, nothing
has disturbed it. Down to the smallest, its pieces make
a chaos of intention, whose outer spirals
loop the galaxies, spool new ones in a quark.

A last stroll through the hamlet, waiting for the plane,
which when I finally see it, is almost here.
It turns, floats down quietly, rolls along the ground,
bouncing like a toy, cuts its engines. We've been told
there's a film crew aboard. Curiosity is high.
In ten minutes I'll be strapped in a seat still warm
from their flight in, but now I stand watching the way
they drop onto the ground, hoping to catch a stray
look of amazement, the shock of first perception.
They look traveled out, weary from sleeping upright
in the same clothes for days, but glad nevertheless, eyes
already working, cigarettes out and lit.

I wonder what version of the place they're after.
Up in back of the hamlet, on a small flat knoll,
the boards are still up for a hockey rink. Hockey,
I think, in a place like this. How strange. Stranger than
movies, than the pile of musk-ox skulls rotting behind
a shed. Than coming upon a live one, alone,
as I was free-forming my way down Greenlander.
It snorted in surprise to have been come upon
quietly, and from above, and so did a half
gallop away from the grassy ledge where it must
have thought it was safe to graze, even to lie down.
The long skirts of its coat swept back and forth across
its hind hoofs, and when it was sure I was no threat,
turned the full crate of its body sideways, a split
river of horn pouring off both sides of its head.
The ummimak—they've even named the school for it—
a gentle, herbivorous, herd-like animal.
This, though, an isolated bull, probably old,
too old to keep up with the rest, and so, content
to spend the rest of its days on a mountainside
not far from a village full of people, dogs, ice,
and the curious dance they do with each other.

I come downstairs at six in the morning. It's dark.
I'm muttering a few words I found at the edge
of sleep, hoping not to forget them. When I do,
I tell them it's all right. Corinna and Ann's lights
are on across the drive. Corinna, I'm sure, has
just come home after a long night of stitching up
the split seams and broken bones of this night's breakdown.
Whatever it was I thought I was looking for
in Grise either wasn't there or disappeared
in the landslide of new sensation. Was that rush.
Even now I can barely keep my eyes on the page.

The sun is beginning to crack the yolk of the day,
and though I put my mind, the hand of my wanting,
down on the still warm body of the memory,
its eyes flutter. I looked around—as I do now—
for something to take with me, but the lights are on
in the kitchen across the way, and though I can
see no one, and it's none of my business, I want
to think the doctor who spent all night picking
splinters of glass out of the flesh of someone's hand
found a few moments alone in her lit kitchen.

The plane that lifted us out of the valley flew
straight into the sky, as though the sky were a part
of earth. I had a small rock in my pocket: gneiss,
Precambrian. That and a fistful of water.
Below us, miles of ice breaking up. Then land. Land
that has never been walked on, land with no trees, land
simmered by water, the melting of glaciers, now
creased by canyons and gorges, memories of flow.

III

The Story Attaches Itself to Us

like the seed of some plant. Its small hooks catch
the cuff of our thought as it walks across
a field. We may not see it or notice
that we are telling some part of it
in telling another story. The story
of Jonah is never about the whale,
who must have been startled one day
to find a two-legged fish in its belly.
So it is, Anangagjuak, you told how
you came upon the body of your wife
lying with her arms reached out, whether
toward you or the life that, though it slowed down,
could no longer wait for her, is not known.
She died looking for you in a storm
as you were hunting, and the snow
buried and preserved her for the day
when you and the others would again
be hunting, when like a dying walrus,
a noise would rise out of your body
at the sight of her on the ground, a noise
you did not know could live there. So I tell
the story of what lives secretly inside us
or comes to be there for no known reason,
and waits only for the day when we
open our mouths in its presence,
and out it comes, alive and chastened,
returned miraculously to the world,
while we turn flukes upward and dive.

Driving North through the Middle of the Continent in Late Fall Looking for Snow

There, at last, the first small tatters of torn cloth scattered
in the shorn fields,
fields folded into themselves, fields outlined in stripped
trumpet vine, black weed, muck of the sort hawks
sit above for hours. The fragment of stained shroud
held between two
pieces of glass in a glass case, freed now

of the body. But on into the dusk, the headlights
spreading under
a sky, wide, descending, brooding over the day's
long hours. Then, on low banks, even the fat
lips of ditches, those facing north, a drape, as at
some spread feast, page
in a book on which nothing is printed,

or, under small clusters of young trees stunned into one
posture for months,
a cloth, wrapping, anything quick to ornament
bleakness or make the eventual seem
accompanied and thick, full of the thing it was.
Night lays calmness
aside, and the first sputtering crackles

of white fire pop out of the air, rushing the headlights,
the plunge forward
into the cataract dark, wind thickening speech.
Swaddled in the hours, we stare down a white
tunnel of thought, and when daylight leaks back, the trees
float out to us,
freed now from fields no longer theirs, or there.

Utitsialangavik

It is not clear whether that is sea
in the background, but I am sure
that in the foreground a group of small stones
gathers around a large upstanding one.
They look like a hungry audience,
anxious to know what the *tunillarvik,*
for that is the name of the upstanding stone,
has to say. They lean forward,
waiting patiently for word.
The tunillarvik has the markings
of deepest veneration (tunillarvik means
“object of veneration”) streaked downward
over its smooth pate. Long strings
of lime-white bird droppings.
For untold eons, gulls have sought this place
as brief refuge from the daily squabble over food
or as perch from which to view
the incremental movement of the hours.
The least and most migratory
of Arctic forms brought together.

Around about, and as far as we can see,
forever, an inhospitable beauty.

“In the old days, we lived on the land.
We carefully followed in the footsteps
of our ancestors. Ever traveling,
we killed every living thing we and our dogs could eat.
Such was our necessity,
living the only life we knew.”

The little congregation of the stones
with its white-haired leader ponders its next move,
perhaps along the *utitsialangavik*
("the pathway one must follow"),
perhaps not.

Mask of the Few Things

This is the mask of getting there,
the mask of wanting a few things
in a bag. This is the bag.
The mask of the wanting
is held in place by a thought,
which you wear at night like a dream.
The dream keeps the dogs in their traces,
the lines untangled, the smoky blur
of the snow in front of you, you
from becoming the ice
of your own desire. Over time, though,
slowly at first, and then less so,
you look for the skidding, the wind,
the dragging over the stones,
the shout like an antler
breaking the surface of skin,
bone come out for a look around,
tooth of the brain, raven
croaking over the mountain,
the yelling into the heart
of frost, blossom cloaked
in the spin of the given.

Whew

The Naskapi once lived along the coast of Labrador. Maybe they still do, but a long time ago, and forever, they loved to tell stories. Only men told them, and only at night. As the people lay in their beds waiting for sleep, the story would begin. At regular intervals, the teller would pause, and the listeners would respond, as though pushing the story along, with a sound something like this: "Eh, eh." If you were standing off a little way in the snow listening, you would first hear a voice carrying a sack of words down a road and then stopping, as if to rest. Then, a small group of voices, as if on cue, would come in like a chorus with "eh, eh." Good, they seemed to be saying, tell us more.

The Naskapi had their big stories, their myths, but everyone preferred the little ones, the "tubaljimun," small tales of everyday life made up on the spot.

Crow said to Peanut, I want you for my bride. Peanut said, Are you kidding? Your beak's too big. Anyway, I am two people. Crow said, Well, fine, I'll have two brides, one for the day, one for the night.

By this time, the children are falling asleep. The little "eh, eh"s slip sideways from their mouths. They are no more than stray windbrushes. The hut made of sticks and caribou hides and spruce boughs and fish bones begins to rise like a loaf of breathing with the smells of sleep and the small hairs across the tops of the toes and the big leggy dreams walking around on the night sky with no clothes on.

No one could have predicted it, but Peanut agreed. Crow, who was no fool, said, Ok, come on, what is it, what do I have to do? Fly to the moon and bring me back a piece of it, she said.

And you know what?

What?

Crow left that day.

I can't believe it.

He still hasn't come back.

Too bad.

It's been ten years in fact, and Peanut, who, as you know, is known for her patience, and waited seven whole years, finally gave up and married Caribou. Caribou promised to stay on the ground.

Well, there it is.

I feel sorry for Crow, though. The moon *is* a long way out there.

Life is real, too.

He should be getting there about now. Whew, he says.

Eh, eh.

Flight of Buntings

It comes in for a landing,
bits of its volatile body
scudding into the snow,
beaks already pecking.
It hops onto the dried spears,
shaking the tiny grains
of last year's anonymous grasses
down onto the whited ground.
Never far from each other,
jitter and scramble, using
the other as radar and scout,
each bird part of a whole
being of bird, bursting,
all of it, at the first hint
of anything moving, becoming
the least bit aware of its
flittering grip on the continuous,
continuously shifting
universe of matter.
And that long scrape
down the mountain's side,
what is it? That never being
still or alone?

for Bert Stern

Reenactment

The picture of the Inuit exhibit at the 1904 St. Louis Exposition shows nineteen people and four dogs on a three-tiered papier-maché platform looking back at the camera as though it, not they, were on exhibit. The man driving the sled on the top platform has his whip arm thrown back. The whip hangs limp in the paper snow. Three of the dogs sit sleepily on their haunches. One of them yawns.

Mouth in a Mouth

Even the full masks split the face,
one part in light, the other shadow.
One eye squinting, the other glaring.
One side of this gash of a mouth grins,
while the other growls. That stuck-out tongue
is a fox, red, with two ears, eyes,
and its own mouth. A long, bent wisp
of plucked ptarmigan down trails
out of the O'd mouth of this other,
forever stunned. Something like snow
falls down one side of its face.
Is that sun on the other? Ice?
A single dog's ear launches off
the head of this one. Are those
stars rattling in the attic?
In back of the masks, a raw gouge
for the face, thin aroma of sap.
You could play the heart of a tree
in there, while the tree pretended
it was cheek sprouting feather, eye
swollen with sight, mouth in a mouth.
But this flesh-pink boy face with two
matching almond eyes and an open
heart-shaped greeting in the mouth,
what whole is he the half of?
What part awaits him, life and death?

Beset

Surrounded with ice, so as to be obliged to remain immovable.

—Sir John Ross, "Explanations of Sea Terms in Icy Seas"

Thrown onto seas few had crossed,
and full of a contemplative's
frenzy. And, wanting to say where
that was, or at least be able
to name the varieties of
endlessness he was in, he broke
ice down. So that, if we ever
found ourselves stranded "on a piece
of ice so large that its extent
cannot be seen," we could write down
in the log we would no doubt keep,
"field." "We are in a field." And so
would have in that place of bonetight
wonder, a word we knew, if no
other familiar, memory
of fields where first we came to lie.
And, if we were ever "surrounded
with ice, so as to be obliged
to remain immovable," we
would turn to the other, saying,
"of course, beset." To be beset
with ice, to be wedged therein, to
want to get up and walk about,
but be told, no, you are beset,
sit down, you are where ice only
is, where you can hear ice whisper
to itself. But about matters
we cannot understand, caught
here in the world and, too,

in the mind, where the world
is most strange because most itself,
we, finally, never again
to not know where that is, or what,
and so be as we are, fixed, here.

Feathers and Fishbone

They wore the masks in the dances,
stepping close together in the same space.
So close they could almost be,
and be called, the same. Were,
in the rituals, always the same.

Some other creature, ptarmigan, bear,
animal they had to persuade out of its skin.
Mimed them in stumbling ways,
ways that their not being what it was
couldn't prevent.

Made fools of themselves, holy fools,
so they could eat. Flapped arms
at the air. Made the sealcrawl
on the floor. To keep the hunting alive.
To be with the rest, hunting.

When the ice groaned and broke
from the shore, they put their boats
in the water and paddled away.
So they could hunt more, sing
to the whale, dying

from the harpoon's sting, as it dragged them
out to sea, perhaps never to return,
down into the sea where the lines tangle
and the lungs burst in a last song
of the air, for which there is no mask,

or one so stuck with feathers and fishbone,
bits of moss and antler and dirt,
it might as well be the one of the world
grinning to be so old and dancing
to the tuneless tune of starlight.

Center of Gravity Rising

Hardy turned the iceberg that sank the *Titanic* into an instrument, an image, of the Imminent Will. "Sinister mate" was his term. Sex was the convulsive act. "Consummation comes, and jars two hemispheres." Freud was thinking of sex when he used the iceberg as image of the place in the mind where we put our uncivil desires. Ice and desire. Ice and secrecy. Glaciers move at different speeds, some an inch a year, others a hundred feet. When the time comes for calving, the biggest births make a twenty-foot wave. Baffin in 1615 reported passing icebergs 240 feet high. That was the part above water. "At night," he said, "we moored our ship to a piece of ice." It was a way to keep from being crushed by it in the dark. An iceberg melts quickest from underneath. As it does, its waist narrows. The top grows heavier. The center of gravity rises from below the water, and at some point, and with no warning, the iceberg rolls over. A crashing slosh, two or three rocking movements, then stillness again.

Half Mask

Maybe it's the half that's there,
the mask itself,
left face or right.

Or, since the wearer,
the carver and wearer,
the painter, is now gone,

it is he or she
who, in being gone,
plays the part

of being both here
and there at the same time,
in and out of the world,

above and below,
half what he is,
half what he wants to be,

walking along a path,
but chatting with the dead
about the snow

beginning to fall at dusk
and the light coming on
in the house across the field.

The dead reassure him.
The dying, too.
He would be lost without them.

The snow comes down
in a way he spends
most of the morning

trying to find words for,
words that would keep it
falling somewhere always.

But the snow keeps falling,
and the carver tires.
Eating and lying down

are part of the thing
he has in mind.
So he leaves the mask unfinished.

When the Stones Revolted

Nothing I know wants nothing, even stones.
I've seen them lying in the riverbed,
exhausted, toward the end of summer,
and the river has thinned down to a film
of pure transparency, when the stones
revolted and rose against the river banks,
which moved against them with such rootedness
and loamy weight, they fell back shouting
to the stars from which they'd come, don't leave us.
Which the stars heard, but only faintly,
and when they shone next, poured down on them
a trickle of something the stones almost
remembered. Though it was a long way off,
and the air was hazy, so they said nothing.

Last Summer of the Century

Cromwell was married in the church next door.
Hard to imagine Cromwell a husband.
Milton is buried there, Frobisher as well.
A hundred feet to the east, a small plaque
where the first bombs fell in 1940.
Gap-toothed fragments of the old city wall
now split new glass high rises with see-through
external elevators. For six weeks,
we took a class as though on a long walk
across a meadow toward a waiting barge.
A flowered barge, with curlicues and ice.
We were to float downriver, not too fast,
and then I suppose into the North Sea
through the mines the Germans put there,
still clutched underwater to their rusting chains.
It was not like that, of course. It was one
brilliant day after another. And then,
a slow surfacing to muffle the kind
of bends you get from coming home fast.
Too fast. From too far away. To a yard
overgrown with weeds, heat like permanent
migraine, windless nights, dirt turned to stone.

We liked the wine bar on the "podium,"
as they called the platform that ran between
the blocks and towers, hairdresser, theatre,
the church with its famous dead, the squared pond.
Very modern. Very 1970.
We sat outside, sipped wine in the sunshine.
When there was sunshine. The barge had a leak,
of course, persistent, and the meadow tilted.
Toward Smithfield Market and the All Bar One.

Men in bloody aprons taking tea break
as the dark-suited masses rushed to work.
It was OK, though. More than OK,
it was Jack London in the morning,
disappearing into "the Abyss,"
Fortnum and Mason's in the afternoon.
What Pound called "the sturdy unkillable
infants of the very poor," dying in fact
before they were thirty, followed by
jars of the greengage plum for Mom, clinging
at eighty-eight to the ledge of her life
above Cherry Creek Parkway and the spare
white mountaintops that ply the western sky.
The creek itself is dry. Has been for years.

It was not easy walking in the city,
but you aren't in London if you don't walk.
We hiked south out of Piccadilly Circus
past a gaggle of international banks,
through dazed bands of day-trippers from small towns
in the Vosges, villages on the upper
Danube, suburbs of Kyoto, Sydney,
Atlanta. Into Waterloo Place, where
heroic posing over the Crimea
clashed with the Gap on Regent Street. Much as
extremities of *The Waste Land* mangled
the need to be in Paris for the weekend.
Wide steps cascaded past the ICA,
into the park Clarissa crosses
in the opening movements of her book.
We would look in vain for the pelicans
we'd seen in the first minutes of the film,
or "sandwich men shuffling and swinging."
On down past the Horse Guards Parade,
the likeness of Viscount Mountbatten
guarding the sandbagged outlet to Downing Street

(terror of the IRA), into the bunker
of another unfinished war, also sandbagged,
under the Foreign Office with its prime
ministerial bed still made, the blundering
and luck palpable in the tight spaces,
recorded wail of the air raid siren,
Churchill addressing still a hushed nation
through its well-mannered proceeding under
the seething rain of fire. Somewhere near
the high held gaze of Florence Nightingale
and the blank-eyed stare of the generic
grieving woman of imperial war,
up under some branches, among car horns,
in the froth of thinking, we came upon
the black glistening statue of Sir John
Franklin. At his feet, on either side
of the pediment, lists of the doomed crews
of the *Erebus* and *Terror*. Who perished
so utterly far from anything displayed
in a park or a shop window, anyone
dying in a doorway of starvation
or bomb dropped in the front garden, one
of whom stood that last summer on the shore
of Queen Maud Gulf perhaps, alone, or with
the two or three of his mates still alive,
glimpsed over a ridge by a native hunter,
but not approached, the shade of whom was found
in a later century and lifted
out of a silence he might have cherished,
watching a few guillemots ruck past,
puffins crash into stony water,
the long horizon and low pebbly beach,
an almost featureless version of the world,
sun like a thin chemise over the cold,
come to seem the anteroom to heaven.

We wound our way up Long Acre, through
the Seven Dials, looking for a cheese store,
one we'd stumbled into the week before.
We forgot it was back among the porn shops
and massage parlors in Soho. And so,
kept walking in the hot afternoon light
in the last summer of the century
toward Ludgate, no longer a circus, and a pint
at The Olde Bell in back of St. Bride's
where, among the shadows and the murmurs,
a man read a novel at the bar.

Such Places

It may have been the eaten shapes of ice
on the rocks facing north that warned us not
to plan too far ahead. Winter would not allow
intervals normal in the spring or fall
for thinking. Roads wound down through trees at dusk
that few trusted, though others, we were sure,
sought such places out, convinced that what
lay quiet under so much snow must know
more than we did. That's why, when the loosening
began and the ice groaned as it rose, cracked
and fell back, no one could not listen long
and not want to be both where they were and where
wherever was to that momentum. It
moved greatly through the trees and then was gone.

This Act

I drive through the unplowed snow around the circle in front of the school I went to more than forty years ago. I do this at a time when no one is there (Christmas), and I do not stop. I fly by and wave, saying, I am somewhere else now. I know you can't see me or hear me (most of you are dead now or, like me, deep down a well of your own digging), but here I am anyway. Ice rings on the road. The streetlights swoon. It was odd being you (it was also glorious), and to mark it, I place this tiny bone fragment, caribou's tibia, carbon-dated back before the last ice age, in the snow by the stone gate. See, I have made a perfect circle in the snow out front in your absence with my little red Toyota. Notice the unwavering arc of the turn, sure grip of the tires, the clean imprint of passage. Forty years. I'm not sure what it is, and, of course, you aren't there to receive it, but here it is anyway. This abstract and peculiar bringing of something back, this glancing over the shoulder at the massive roof.

The Sandhill Cranes Come Back

I start to sense in some place
other than the ear the thin,
high, ululating wail, and
for a minute, I think the wind
has found a razor's slip in the jambs.
Then memory blinks its shutter,
eyeball of iguana, and I know. Again.
Fine wire at the back of the brain.
The sound that every spring
wakes the snow, that woke whatever stone
it was that first wanted lichen for a mate,
sound that makes wailing into song,
one sung together at great height
or alone when you can't reach the reason
or the words. When words almost capitulate.
Late November, branches twisting up the sky.

Notes

"First Mask": Several of the mask poems draw on images in Ann Feinup-Riordon's *The Living Tradition of Yup'ik Masks: Agayuliyararput: Our Way of Making Prayer* (1996).

"Thule": Elements in the poem came from looking through Vilhjalmur Stephansson, *Ultima Thule: Further Mysteries of the Arctic* (1994), *The Geography of Strabo,* 8 vols., trans. H. L. James (1917), and Moses Hadas, *A History of Greek Literature* (1950).

"Lichen": Certain facts here came from *The Lichens,* ed. Vernon Ahmadjian and Mason Hale (1973), as well as *Northern Survival: A Practical Guide to Survival in the Northern Regions, Prepared by the Employment and Related Services Division, Department of Indian Affairs and Northern Development* (1972).

"The Deaths of William Braine": See Owen Beattie and John Geiger, *Frozen in Time: The Fate of the Franklin Expedition* (1998). For the Inuit behavior toward the expedition, see David C. Woodman's *Unraveling the Franklin Mystery* (1992) and *Strangers Among Us* (1995).

"The Other Side of the Air": See Don E. Dumond, *The Eskimos and Aleuts* (1977).

"You Look Out": See Roland Huntford, *Nansen: The Explorer as Hero* (2002).

"Not a Record": See Ann Feinup-Riordan's *The Living Tradition of Yup'ik Masks: Agayuliyararput: Our Way of Making Prayer* (1996).

"Last Three Minutes": See D. C. W. Davies, *The Last Three Minutes* (1994).

"Grise": The Inuit testimony was taken from *The High Arctic Relocation: Summary of Supporting Evidence* (Ottawa: Royal Commission on Aboriginal Peoples, 1994). The best source for information on and pictures of inukshuks is Norman Hallendy, *Inuksuit: Silent Messengers of the Arctic* (2000).

"The Story Attaches Itself to Us": The story of Anangagjuak is told by Knud Rasmussen in *Across Arctic America* (1927).

"Utitsialangavik": This poem begins by describing one of the inukshuks in Norman Hallendy's *Inuksuit* (2000).

"Beset": See Sir John Ross, *A Voyage of Discovery, Made under the Orders of the Admiralty . . . for the Purpose of Exploring Baffin's Bay, and Enquiring into the Probability of a North-West Passage,* 2 vols. (1819).

"Center of Gravity Rising": The Thomas Hardy poem is "The Convergence of the Twain." For the comment by Baffin, see *Narratives of Voyages towards the North-West, in Search of a Passage to Cathay and India, 1492–1631,* selected by Thomas Rundell (1849).

Acknowledgments

I would like to thank the editors of the following journals where some of these poems or versions of them were originally published: *Amicus Journal* (now *OnEarth*): "The Sandhill Cranes Come Back"; *Denver Quarterly*: "In the Art Museum Coffee Shop"; *5AM*: "Mask on Mask" and "The Other Side of the Air"; *The Flying Island*: "This Act"; *Green Mountains Review*: "White Winged Swarming"; *Hamilton Stone Review*: "Dream Seed," "Museum," "Utitsialangavik," and "Half Mask"; *New American Writing*: "Thule"; *The Ohio Review*: "First Mask" and "Mask of the Few Things"; *Organization and Environment*: "Driving North Through the Middle of the Continent in Late Fall Looking for Snow," "Above Bow Lake," "Dream Seed," and "Crocus, Beginning"; *Rattle*: "Beset"; *River Styx*: "Last Summer of the Century"; *Spoon River Poetry Review*: "Lichen"; *Tar River Poetry*: "The Story Attaches Itself to Us"; *West Branch*: "The Stones at Callinish, Isle of Lewis," "The Deaths of William Braine," and "Grise."

"Whew" was first published in *The Talking of Hands: Unpublished Writings by New Rivers Press Authors,* ed. Robert Alexander et al. (1998). "Mask of the Few Things" was republished in *The Ohio Review, Thirtieth Anniversary,* 1971–2001*: New & Selected,* Vol. II (2001). "Thule" was republished in *The World's Best Poetry/ Poem Finder,* Roth Publishing, Inc. [electronic]. "Last Summer of the Century" won the 2001 *River Styx* International Poetry Contest.

Thanks to The Arctic Institute of North America at the University of Calgary for putting the institute's research facilities at my disposal for two weeks during the summer of 1995, to Indiana University for providing me a Summer Faculty Research Fellowship, to the Indiana Arts Commission for a fellowship to assist my travel to the High Arctic, to the National Endowment for the Arts, to the New York Foundation for the Arts, to Yaddo for a residency, and as so often, to The Ragdale Foundation for several residencies, where many of these poems were drafted and/or polished.

Special thanks, too, to the following who have helped this project along with some extremely useful critical enthusiasm: Christopher Cokinos, Elizabeth Dodd, Tam Lin Neville, Jim Scrimgeour, Bert Stern, David Wojahn, and Dean Young. Elton Glaser of The University of Akron Press engineered the best rethinking of a manuscript I've ever been through. Many thanks to him. To Dorian, of course, whose encouragement and editorial skills have left their mark on every page.